# 聰明的園丁 上

## Wisdom from the Word

### 發現比喻的奧祕

作者・洪善美　／　繪者・李明先、林智勇、莫卡

國家圖書館出版品預行編目 (CIP) 資料

聰明的園丁：發現比喻的奧祕 / 洪善美作；李明先
等繪 . -- 初版 . -- 臺北市：時兆，2018.09
　　冊；　公分
　ISBN 978-986-6314-80-3( 全套：精裝 )

1. 聖經故事　2. 比喻

241.68　　　　　　　　　　　　107010673

聰明的園丁　上　發現比喻的奧祕
Wisdom from the Word

作者｜洪善美
繪者｜李明先、林智勇、莫卡

董事長｜金時英
發行人｜周英弼
出版者｜時兆出版社
服務專線｜886-2-27726420
傳真｜886-2-27401448
地址｜台北市10556八德路二段410巷5弄1號2樓
網址｜www.stpa.org
電子信箱｜stpa@ms22.hinet.net

主編｜周麗娟
責任編輯｜由鈺涵
校對｜林思慧、陳美如
封面設計｜邵信成
內頁設計｜邵信成、李宛青
法律顧問｜宏鑑律師事務所　電話 886-2-27150270

商業書店總經銷｜聯合發行股份有限公司 TEL: 886-2-29178022
基督教書房｜基石音樂有限公司 TEL: 886-2-29625951
網路商店｜store.pchome.com.tw/stpa

ISBN｜978-986-6314-80-3（全套：精裝）
定價｜新台幣1200元（上下冊不拆售）
出版日期｜2018年9月 初版一刷

Original Korean & English edition copyright©2018 by Korean Publishing House

www.stpa.org

請掃 QR code
進入時兆官網
點選左側「免費會員專區」
填寫資料加入會員後
再點選左側「影音專區」
即可線上聽故事

聰明的園丁 上
Wisdom from the Word
發現比喻的奧祕

大衛：媽咪，湯米每次都欺負我。
　　　他每天搶我的東西還打我。
　　　他真是個大壞蛋。
　　　我下次也要這樣對付他！

媽媽：大衛，看來你真的很生氣。
　　　在你想要對付湯米之前，
　　　媽媽先說個故事給你聽，好嗎？

**David:** Mommy, Tommy always bullies me. He takes my stuff and hits me every day. He is such a bad guy. I'm going to do the same to him next time!

**Mom:** David, you seem really upset, but before you treat him that way, I'd like to tell you a story. Okay?

# 麥子與稗子
## The Wheat and the Tares

耶穌又設個比喻對他們說：「天國好像人撒好種在田裡，
及至人睡覺的時候，有仇敵來，將稗子撒在麥子裡就走了。
到長苗吐穗的時候，稗子也顯出來。
田主的僕人來告訴他說：『主啊，你不是撒好種在田裡嗎？從哪裡來的稗子呢？』
主人說：『這是仇敵做的。』僕人說：『你要我們去薅出來嗎？』
主人說：『不必，恐怕薅稗子，連麥子也拔出來。
容這兩樣一齊長，等著收割。當收割的時候，我要對收割的人說，先將稗子薅出來，捆成捆，留著燒；惟有麥子要收在倉裡。』
（馬太福音13：24－30）

春天來了，春雨也開始下了。
「僕人們！播種的季節到了，我們去田裡耕作吧！」
充滿智慧、心胸寬大又有錢的地主說。

Spring came and it began to rain.
"Servants! It's time to plant the seeds. Let's plow the field!" said the rich landlord who was known for his wisdom and generosity.

地主和他的僕人們懷著激動的心情，
在廣闊的麥田裡細心地播種。

The landlord and his servants were full of excitement,
they sowed the seeds carefully in the wide field.

過了幾天以後，
在田裡工作的一個僕人，氣喘吁吁地跑去找地主。

A few days later,
a servant working in the field ran to the landlord, panting.

8

「主人哪！不好了，不好了！麥田裡長出很多稗子的苗了！」僕人大聲地說。

「稗子的苗？」

「主人，我們該怎麼辦呢？要是放著它不管的話，麥苗的水分和養分就會被稗子搶走了！

我們馬上去把稗子拔出來嗎？」

「不，先留著它們吧！」

「咦？您的意思是不用管它們？」

"Master! Something bad happened! There are lots of tares growing among the wheat!" said the servant loudly.

"Tares?"

"What should we do, master? If we let the tares grow, they will take away water and nutrients from the wheat!

Should we pluck them out?"

"No, just leave them as they are!"

"What? You want them to grow in the field?"

「是的，現在要區別稗子和麥子的苗並不容易，
如果不小心的話，就會連麥子一起拔掉了。
等它們都長大成熟，到那時候你就很容易區分什麼是麥子，什麼是稗子了！」
「主人，我知道了。」
雖然他們現在很擔心，但也沒有其他方法了，只能等到收成的時候。

"Yes. It is hard to tell the tares from wheat at this time.
You might pluck out wheat accidentally, if you are not careful.
So leave them until the harvest. When the time comes, it will be easy to tell them apart."
"Okay, master."
Although they were worried, they had no choice but to wait until the harvest.

麥子和稗子一天天的長大了。
麥子因為吸收陽光的照射、充足的水分和營養，結出一顆顆飽滿的麥穗，
稗子也很努力地一點一點地長高。

As time went by, the tares and the wheat grew gradually.
The wheat absorbed the sunlight, water and nutrients and turned into healthy crops,
while the tares also tried very hard to grow taller.

終於來到了收割的季節。
黃澄澄的麥子壓彎了麥稈的腰，
而稗子卻像挺直腰桿的軍人，站在麥田中。

Finally, it was time for the harvest.
The golden wheat bent over
while the tares stood still like soldiers in the field.

當準備開始收割時，
地主對僕人說：
「大家先把稗子收一收，捆成一捆捆的，然後燒了。
之後再把收好的麥子存在穀倉裡。」

僕人們一邊燒著稗子一邊說：
「在春天撒種的時候，主人告訴我們不要拔掉稗子，他說的話果然是對的。」
「是啊！我們差一點就把麥苗也拔起來了。
雖然那時候很擔心，但還好我們忍下來了。」

When the harvest eventually came,
the landlord said to the servants,
"Guys, pluck out the tares. Bundle them first and burn them all.
After that, gather the wheat into the barn."

The servants said as they were burning the tares,
"It's good that we listened to the master when he told us not to pluck out the tares in spring."
"I agree! We would have plucked out the wheat, too.
Even though we were worried then, it was good that we waited."

「大衛，去郊遊時，你對什麼事情最感興趣？」

「我最喜歡尋寶遊戲！我用棍子撥開落葉，仔細尋找，然後搬開大石頭找，但都沒有找到，後來在我的包包底下找到銅板了！」

「這樣子啊！你想不想知道找到真正寶物的祕訣呢？」

"David, what do you like the most about hiking?"

"I love treasure hunts! Once I looked through the fallen leaves with a stick and lift up a huge rock to search for a coin, but in the end I found it under my bag!"

"I see. Do you want to know the secret of finding the real treasure?"

# 隱藏的寶物
## The Hidden Treasure

天國好像寶貝藏在地裡,人遇見了就把它藏起來,歡歡喜喜地去變賣一切所有的,買這塊地。
（馬太福音13：44）

很久以前，在加利利的某個村莊裡，有一塊荒廢很久的田地。
那是一塊布滿了各種粗糙石頭的田地。

「怎麼有這麼多的石頭啊？我連一點可以種田的地方也沒有！」
那些原本租地要來種田的農夫們，嘴上發著牢騷，並很快地就放棄了種田的工作。

A long time ago, in a village called Galilee,
there was a long-abandoned rocky field.

"How come there are so many rocks in the field! There is no place I can farm."
The farmers who rented the land to grow crops complained and gave up very soon.

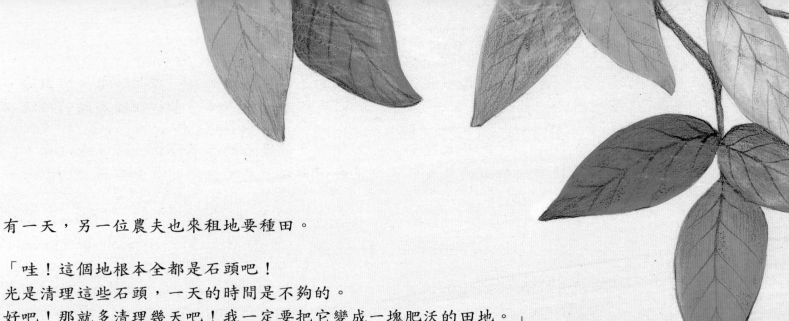

有一天，另一位農夫也來租地要種田。

「哇！這個地根本全都是石頭吧！
光是清理這些石頭，一天的時間是不夠的。
好吧！那就多清理幾天吧！我一定要把它變成一塊肥沃的田地。」

**鏗鏗！鏘鏘！**
雖然農夫的汗水像雨水一樣地流下來，但他並沒有放下手中的鋤頭繼續工作。

One day, another farmer came to rent the field.

"Wow, it is full of rocks here! I can't clean the field in just one day.
Ok then, let me spend a few more days to do it. I will not give up until I make it a good field."

**Clank! Clank!**
The farmer was sweating up a storm, but he didn't put down the hoe in his hands.

就在那個時候，
**鏗鏘！**
鋤頭敲到了什麼東西！

Right at that moment,
**Clank!**
The hoe hit something!

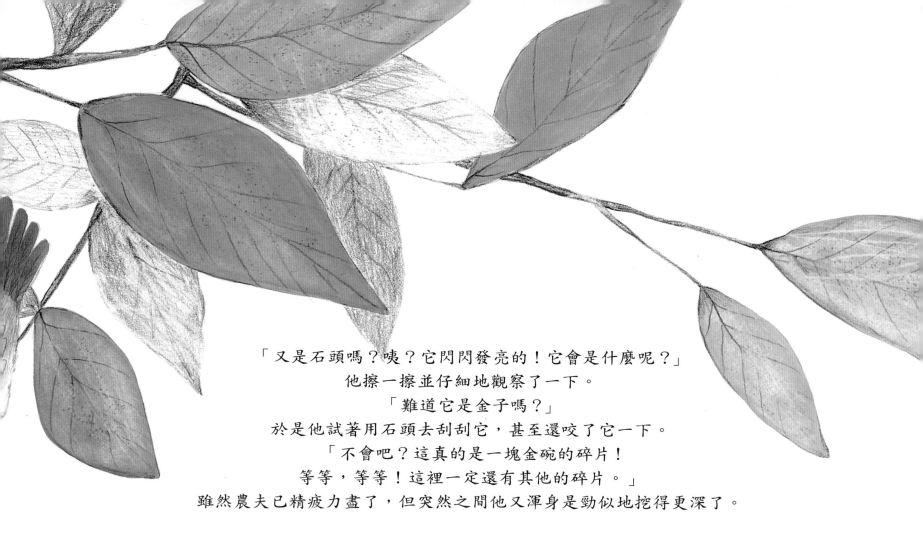

「又是石頭嗎？咦？它閃閃發亮的！它會是什麼呢？」
他擦一擦並仔細地觀察了一下。
「難道它是金子嗎？」
於是他試著用石頭去刮刮它，甚至還咬了它一下。
「不會吧？這真的是一塊金碗的碎片！
等等，等等！這裡一定還有其他的碎片。」
雖然農夫已精疲力盡了，但突然之間他又渾身是勁似地挖得更深了。

**鏘鏘！**「找到了！這一定就是碗的底部！」**鏘鏘！**「這個是手把！」
農夫按捺住內心的激動，他想了一想：「這樣不行，我乾脆把這塊地買下來。」

"Is it another rock? But it's shiny! What is this?"
He rubbed it and took a closer look.
"Is this gold?"
He tried to scratch it with a rock and even bit it.
"What? This is a real piece of a golden bowl!
Okay, hold on! There must be some other pieces of the bowl here."
Although he was exhausted, he was suddenly revived and dug deeper into the ground.

**Clank!** "I found it! This must be the bottom part of the bowl." **Clank!** "This is the handle!"
As he tried to calm down, he thought, "This is not a good idea, I should just buy the whole field."

農夫急忙跑回家，變賣了所有的家產，他一定要買那塊石頭地。

「老公，不可以！你難道瘋了嗎？
為了那塊沒有用的石頭地，你竟然賣掉一切？
喔！不！我們家要完蛋了，天呀！」老婆嗚嗚地哭著。

「老婆，別擔心！
那塊地可不是沒有用的石頭地。它是一塊寶藏之地呢！」
農夫急忙安慰老婆。

He hurried back home and sold everything he had to buy the rocky field.

"No, my dear! Are you insane?
Are you selling everything for just that useless rocky field?
My goodness! How are we going to live? Oh no!" his wife wept.

"Don't worry, honey!
That field is not useless. It has treasure in it!"
he tried to comfort her.

買了地的農夫開始在石頭地的各個角落挖掘，
每挖一次，就有新的寶物出現。
很快地，他變成了一個有錢人。

還有令人更開心的消息呢！
當他為了尋找寶物而不斷挖掘石頭地時，
因為石頭都被除掉了，這塊地變成肥沃的好地，
今年反而成為一個五穀豐收的好年。

After he bought the field, the farmer searched every part of it.
Whenever he dug a little deeper, new treasure was found.
Soon, he became a wealthy man.

And there was more good news.
As he dug to find the treasure,
the rocks were also moved away, so the field became fertile.
It turned out to be a year of good harvest.

在奶奶七十大壽的宴會上，大衛唱歌給奶奶聽。
但是突然之間他忘詞了！
他不知道該怎麼辦，就號啕大哭了。

「怎麼辦？哇嗚！」

媽媽告訴過他要認真練習唱歌的，
現在他很後悔沒有聽媽媽的話。

David sang for his grandma at her 70th birthday party.
But he suddenly forgot the lyrics!
He didn't know what to do, so he cried.

"What am I going to do? Wa-a-a!"

His mommy had told him to practice many times.
Now he regrets that he didn't listen.

# 十個伴娘
## Ten Bridesmaids

「那時，天國好比十個童女拿著燈出去迎接新郎。
其中有五個是愚拙的，五個是聰明的。
愚拙的拿著燈，卻不預備油；
聰明的拿著燈，又預備油在器皿裡。
新郎遲延的時候，她們都打盹，睡著了。
半夜有人喊著說：『新郎來了，你們出來迎接他！』
那些童女就都起來收拾燈。
愚拙的對聰明的說：『請分點油給我們，因為我們的燈要滅了。』
聰明的回答說：『恐怕不夠你我用的；不如你們自己到賣油的那裡去買吧！』
她們去買的時候，新郎到了。那預備好了的，同他進去坐席，門就關了。
其餘的童女隨後也來了，說：『主啊，主啊，給我們開門！』
他卻回答說：『我實在告訴你們，我不認識你們。』
所以，你們要警醒；因為那日子，那時辰，你們不知道。」

（馬太福音25：1－13）

傍晚的時候，新娘的家裡點上了油燈，一瞬間燈火通明，變得像白天一樣。
十位伴娘們感到非常地興奮。

「我很好奇新郎長得怎麼樣！好想趕快看到他哦！」
「我也是！啊！我的心情好緊張哦！」
「我們現在趕快出去吧！新郎來的時間就快到了！」
「好的！你們的油燈都帶了嗎？」

十個伴娘拿著油燈出去等候新郎的到來。
為了迎接新郎，她們用油燈把街道照得非常明亮。

In the evening, the bride's home was lit with oil lamps and it turned as bright as daytime.
The ten bridesmaids were excited.

"I wonder how the groom looks! I want to meet him as soon as possible!"
"Me too! Ah, I'm so nervous!"
"Let's go out now! It's almost time for him to come!"
"Okay! Did you all take the oil lamps?"

The ten bridesmaids took the oil lamps,
waiting for the groom.
They lit up the dark streets
to greet the groom.

時間一點一滴的流逝，深夜也悄悄地來臨。

「新郎為什麼到現在都還沒有來？」
「他應該已在路上了吧？啊……，好睏！我快要睡著了！」
**呼嚕…呼嚕……**
十個伴娘又累又睏，等著等著……不知不覺的就睡著了。

不知過了多久，半夜中忽然聽到了聲響。
「新郎來了！新郎來了！大家快出來迎接他！」

Time passed and it was late at night.

"Why isn't he coming yet?"
"Is he even on his way? Ah…I'm getting sleepy!"
**Z-z-z-z-z-z-z.**
The ten bridesmaids became drowsy and fell asleep as they waited.

Then at midnight, they heard something.
"The groom is coming! The groom is coming! Come out to meet him!"

「那是新郎！他來了！」十個伴娘從睡夢中驚醒，站了起來。

「大事不妙了！我的油燈快要熄滅了！」

油燈如果熄滅的話，她們就不能接待新郎。

其中五個伴娘正好多準備了一些油，馬上就把油加到快熄滅的油燈裡。

"Here comes the groom! He is coming!" The ten bridesmaids were startled and got up instantly.

"Oh no! My oil lamp is dying out!"

They couldn't greet the groom if the lamps were out.

Five of the bridesmaids happen to had prepared extra oil so they re-filled their lamps.

「你們能不能也分給我們一點油？」
另外五個沒有多準備油的伴娘，心裡焦急地不斷直跺腳。
「對不起，我的油只夠點亮我自己的油燈。」有油的那五個伴娘，每個人都這樣說。
「你們現在為何不趕快去買油回來？」
那五個伴娘拿著已經熄滅的油燈，向著賣油鋪奔去。

"Would you share some oil with us?"
The other five bridesmaids who hadn't prepared extra oil were stamping their feet anxiously.
"Sorry, I only have enough to light up my own lamp," said those who had extra oil.
"Why don't you go and buy some oil now?"
The five bridesmaids ran to the store with their lamps that had gone out already.

新郎帶著那五位等待他的伴娘，朝著他的家走去。

**咚咚咚……叭叭叭！叮叮叮……噹噹噹……鏘鏘鏘！**

走在路上的迎親隊伍，喜氣洋洋地吹奏著樂器，聲音響徹了大街小巷。

那五個有事先準備油的聰明伴娘，拿著油燈一起走進了已預備好婚宴的新郎家中。

The groom took the five remaining bridesmaids to his house.

**Tralala- toot- toot- toot, ding-ding-ding, Jingle-jangle, clank-clank-clank!**

The procession played the instruments joyfully and the sound reverberated in the streets.

The five clever bridesmaids who had prepared the oil in advance went into the groom's house,

where the wedding party was ready.

另外去買油的五個伴娘，
過了很久氣喘吁吁地跑回來，但已經太遲了！
**叩叩叩……叩叩叩……叩叩叩！**
「請你們開開門，讓我們進去，好嗎？」
「你們是誰呢？那些準備好的客人們都全部進來了。」
大門被緊緊的關著，沒辦法打開。

那五個愚蠢的伴娘站在漆黑的街道上，難過地哭了起來。
「唉……唉！！！打扮這麼漂亮有什麼用啊！」
「早知道我就早一點起來，先把油預備好！」她們啜泣地說。

The five bridesmaids who went to buy the oil came back,
running and out of breath, but they were too late.
**Knock-knock-knock! Knock-knock-knock!**
"Would you please open the door to let us in?"
"Who are you? The guests have already come in."
The door was shut tight and couldn't be opened.

The five foolish bridesmaids stood sadly and cried in the dark street.
"Ahhh!!! We dressed up but it's of no use!"
"I should have woken up a little earlier to prepare some more oil!" they whimpered.

爸爸：艾蜜莉！你練完琴了嗎？
艾蜜莉：剛才都練完了。
爸爸：是嗎？我只聽到兩三次琴聲而已。
艾蜜莉：老師說我彈得很好，我有信心！
爸爸：是哦！艾蜜莉，明天就是妳的發表會了，
　　　我建議妳要多練習幾次。
艾蜜莉：我待會兒再彈啦！

接著，艾蜜莉一溜煙地跑進了房間。

**Daddy:** Emily! Have you finished practicing the piano?
**Emily:** Yes, I have.
**Daddy:** Oh yeah? I only heard it a few times, though.
**Emily:** The teacher told me that I'm good at it.
　　　　I am confident of myself!
**Daddy:** I don't know, Emily.
　　　　For your performance tomorrow,
　　　　I suggest you practice a little more.
**Emily:** I will do it later!

Then Emily popped into her room.

# 三個僕人
**Three servants**

「天國又好比一個人要往外國去，就叫了僕人來，把他的家業交給他們，
按著各人的才幹給他們銀子：一個給了五千，一個給了二千，一個給了一千，就往外國去了。
那領五千的隨即拿去做買賣，另外賺了五千。
那領二千的也照樣另賺了二千。
但那領一千的去掘開地，把主人的銀子埋藏了。
過了許久，那些僕人的主人來了，和他們算帳。
那領五千銀子的又帶著那另外的五千來，說：『主啊，你交給我五千銀子。請看，我又賺了五千。』
主人說：『好，你這又良善又忠心的僕人，你在不多的事上有忠心，我要把許多事派你管理；可以進來享受你主人的快樂。』
那領二千的也來，說：『主啊，你交給我二千銀子。請看，我又賺了二千。』
主人說：『好，你這又良善又忠心的僕人，你在不多的事上有忠心，我要把許多事派你管理；可以進來享受你主人的快樂。』
那領一千的也來，說：『主啊，我知道你是忍心的人，沒有種的地方要收割，沒有散的地方要聚斂，
我就害怕，去把你的一千銀子埋藏在地裡。請看，你的原銀子在這裡。』
主人回答說：『你這又惡又懶的僕人，你既知道我沒有種的地方要收割，沒有散的地方要聚斂，
就當把我的銀子放給兌換銀錢的人，到我來的時候，可以連本帶利收回。
奪過他這一千來，給那有一萬的。
因為凡有的，還要加給他，叫他有餘；沒有的，連他所有的也要奪過來。
把這無用的僕人丟在外面黑暗裡；在那裡必要哀哭切齒了。』」

**（馬太福音25：14－30）**

一他連得≒新台幣一千五百萬元
A talent equals approximately NTD15,000,000.

42

有一個主人要去遙遠的國家旅行。
離開之前他把三個僕人叫來，給他們一人一個袋子。
一個袋子裡裝了五個他連得＊，另一個袋子裡有兩個他連得，
最後一個袋子則裝了一個他連得。
「好多錢喔！為什麼主人給我們這麼大的一筆錢呢？」
「我不在的期間，你們要好好管理這些錢。」

A master had to travel to a country far away.
So before he left, he gathered his three servants and gave each of them a bag.
In one bag there were 5 talents, another bag 2 talents, and the other bag 1 talent.
"This is a lot of money! Why are you giving it to us, master?"
"Take care of it while I am gone."

主人前腳一離開，得到一個他連得的僕人就開始發牢騷。
「哎喲！真頭痛！為什麼要吩咐我們做這種事呢？」
「為什麼？不會啊！我覺得很高興！這不就表示主人很信任我們！」
得到五個他連得和兩個他連得的僕人，因此更充滿活力地去工作了。

Once the master left, the servant who received 1 talent started complaining.
"Ahh! It's giving me a headache. Why did he give us money?"
"Why? It's fine. I am actually happy. It means that he trusts us!"
The servants who received 5 talents and 2 talents went out to work,
feeling energetic.

「這該怎麼辦？」
「如果我一個不小心把錢弄丟了，會被主人狠狠地教訓一頓的！
嗯！我想還是挖一個洞，把錢藏在地底下最安全了。」

"What should I do?"
"If I do something wrong with it, I will lose it all and my master will be mad at me.
Oh well, I think I'd better dig a hole in the ground and bury the money for it is the safest way to store it."

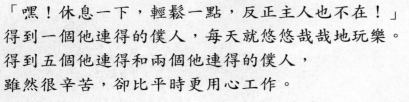

「嘿！休息一下，輕鬆一點，反正主人也不在！」
得到一個他連得的僕人，每天就悠悠哉哉地玩樂。
得到五個他連得和兩個他連得的僕人，
雖然很辛苦，卻比平時更用心工作。

"Hey, the master is not here anyway. Let's take a break and relax!"
The servant who received 1 talent was idled and had fun every day,
while the servants who received 5 talents and 2 talents
worked even harder despite the tiredness.

某天，主人在沒有通知僕人的情況下，突然回來了。
「這些日子沒發生什麼事情吧？我給你們的他連得都怎麼管理呢？」
「主人，我努力工作，我用這五個他連得，又另外賺了五個他連得！」
「很好，你辛苦了！這十個他連得就給你做為獎勵了。」
「主人，我用得到的兩個他連得，又另外賺了兩個他連得。」
「太棒了！我同樣也把這四個他連得給你做為獎賞。」

One day, without letting the servants know, the master came back.
"How was everything? What happened to the talents I gave you?"
"Master! With the 5 talents I got, I worked very hard to double the amount!"
"Good job! I will give you 10 talents as a reward."
"Master! With the 2 talents I received, I made 2 more talents."
"Great! I will give you 4 talents as a reward as well."

那個得到一個他連得的僕人，
也來到主人的面前，說：
「主人，我不知道該怎麼做，
又怕把這一個他連得弄丟了，
所以，就把它埋在地底下。
這是你交給我的一個他連得。」

Then the servant who received 1 talent
stepped up to the master, saying,
"Master! I didn't know what to do,
and I was afraid that I might lose it,
so I hid it well under the ground.
Here is the 1 talent you gave me."

「什麼？你不就跟小偷沒兩樣！
我不在的這段期間，你什麼事都不做，整天吃喝玩樂。
來人啊！馬上把這懶惰無能的僕人趕出去！」
主人就拿走他手中的一個他連得，
給了那又另外賺得五個他連得的僕人。

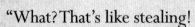

"What? That's like stealing!
That means you didn't work at all while I was away.
Kick this lazy and useless servant out of my house!"
Then the master took away the 1 talent he had given to the lazy servant
and gave it to the servant who had earned 5 extra talents.

「哎喲，早知道我就應該努力工作！」
被趕出去的僕人非常後悔，
只能看著另外兩個僕人賺得獎賞的快樂樣子了。

"Oh no! I should have worked hard."
The servant regretted his laziness,
as he looked at the two servants
who were delighted with their rewards.

51

艾蜜莉：好！快好了啦！我就快要贏得比賽了！可是爸爸、媽媽一直嘮叨！手要洗乾淨，要記得刷牙，要打掃房間，東西要放回原處，要常常吃蔬菜，要多看不同的書。他們甚至不讓我看那些我想看的電視節目。

爸爸：艾蜜莉，爸爸、媽媽這樣做都是為你好。

**Emily:** I was almost there! I almost won the contest! But mommy and daddy are always nagging! They tell me to wash my hands, brush my teeth, clean up, put things back where they are supposed to be. They tell me to eat vegetables more often and read various books. They don't even let me watch the TV programs I like.

**Daddy:** Emily, It's all for your own good.

# 撒種的人
**The Sower**

祂用比喻對他們講許多道理，說：「有一個撒種的出去撒種；
撒的時候，有落在路旁的，飛鳥來吃盡了；
有落在土淺石頭地上的，土既不深，發苗最快，
日頭出來一曬，因為沒有根，就枯乾了；
有落在荊棘裡的，荊棘長起來，把它擠住了；
又有落在好土裡的，就結實，有一百倍的，有六十倍的，有三十倍的。
有耳可聽的，就應當聽！」
**（馬太福音13：3－9）**

陽光燦爛的一天，
農夫正在田裡撒種。
有一顆種子咕嚕咕嚕地滾到馬路上了。

It was a sunny day
and a farmer was scattering seeds all around the field.
One seed rolled and fell on the road.

硬梆梆的馬路一邊玩著吃灰塵的遊戲，
一邊抱怨著炙熱的陽光。
「你好！如果你讓我在這裡長大的話，
我會發芽，然後長成一棵大樹，很快地我就能幫你遮蔭哦！」種子說。
「你在說什麼？我不需要樹來遮蔭，閃一邊去！」

The hard ground was busy playing the game of eating the dust
and complaining about the burnning sun.
"Hi! If you would accept me,
I will sprout and become a tree to make shade for you soon."
"What are you talking about? I don't need a tree. Go away!"

啊呀！種子難過地哇哇大哭起來。

這時，麻雀拍動著翅膀從高處飛了過來，

**啪啪啪……啪啪啪！**

「哇！那是一顆美味可口的種子耶！」麻雀馬上就一口吃掉了種子。

掉在路上的種子，還來不及發芽就被吃掉了。

The seed was sad and cried.

But then, a sparrow fluttered over.

**Flap ……Flap!**

"Wow! That is a delicious seed!" The sparrow ate it immediately.

The seed on the road was eaten even before it could sprout.

「哇！我發芽了！嘻！嘻！我的根……噹啷…噹啷…長出來了！」
在石頭地上的那顆種子非常興奮。
但是沒多久，砰的一聲！它的根部就撞上了一個東西。
原來它被地底下的一顆大石頭給擋住了。

「石頭先生， 你可以讓出一條路，給我的根通過嗎？我需要水分的。」
「什麼？你的意思是叫我把自己打破，變成兩半嗎？
我可是在石頭中長得最帥的一個！絕對不行！」

"Wow! I sprouted! Hee-hee! Here's my root! Ta-da-!"
The seed on the rocky road got so excited.
But soon after, bang! The root hit something.
It was blocked by a big rock under the ground.

"Mr. Rock, would you mind to sparing some space to let my root grow? I need some water."
"What? So are you asking me to break myself?
I am the best-looking rock ever! Never!"

石頭冷漠無情地馬上阻擋了根的成長，
所以，剛發芽的種子最後就枯死了。

The rocky road rejected the seed,
so the newly sprouted seed dried up and died.

59

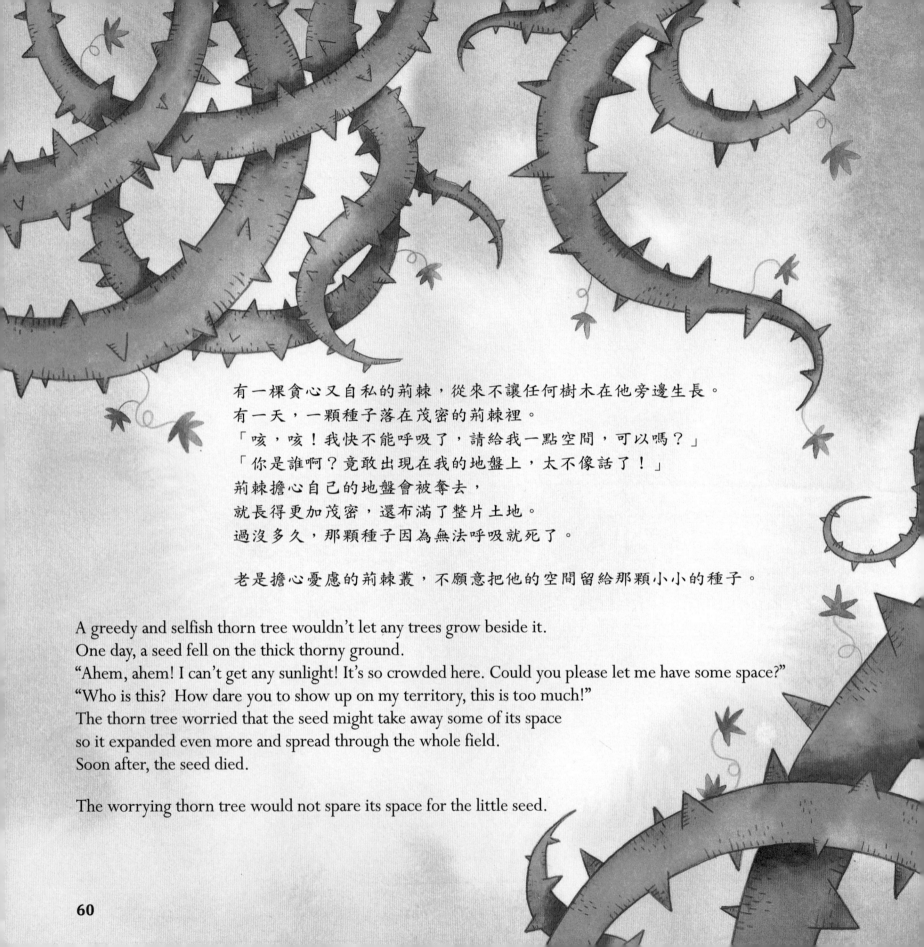

有一棵貪心又自私的荊棘，從來不讓任何樹木在他旁邊生長。
有一天，一顆種子落在茂密的荊棘裡。
「咳，咳！我快不能呼吸了，請給我一點空間，可以嗎？」
「你是誰啊？竟敢出現在我的地盤上，太不像話了！」
荊棘擔心自己的地盤會被奪去，
就長得更加茂密，還布滿了整片土地。
過沒多久，那顆種子因為無法呼吸就死了。

老是擔心憂慮的荊棘叢，不願意把他的空間留給那顆小小的種子。

A greedy and selfish thorn tree wouldn't let any trees grow beside it.
One day, a seed fell on the thick thorny ground.
"Ahem, ahem! I can't get any sunlight! It's so crowded here. Could you please let me have some space?"
"Who is this? How dare you to show up on my territory, this is too much!"
The thorn tree worried that the seed might take away some of its space
so it expanded even more and spread through the whole field.
Soon after, the seed died.

The worrying thorn tree would not spare its space for the little seed.

「是誰啊？」

"Who is this?"

61

咚！

「哦？哇！好漂亮的一顆種子呀！我一定會好好的照顧你的。」

這塊好田地非常呵護這顆種子，就把最好的東西都給他，讓他可以好好地長大。

種子努力忍受風吹雨打的天氣，

在不知不覺中就長成了一棵大樹。

要收成的秋天來了，

大樹的枝子上結滿了許許多多的果子。

**Dong!**

"Huh? Wow! This is one pretty seed! I will take care of you."

The good land let the seed have everything it needed to grow.

The seed endured windy and severe weather.

Then finally, it became a big tree.

When it was almost the harvest season,

the tree was full of fruits.

「哇！哈哈哈！」
好心的田地因為這棵大樹的收成，感到滿心歡暢。
哼著歌曲的農夫也開心地整天呵呵笑呢！

**"Wow! Ha-ha-ha!"**
The good land was so glad about the tree's harvest that he felt like he could fly.
The farmer also whistled and was tickled with joy all day!

艾蜜莉想要買一個漂亮的洋娃娃，
所以她不斷的存錢。
但是存錢卻沒有如她想像中的那麼容易。
因為就算她很想要吃點零食或喝些飲料，都必須忍住。

「不要買洋娃娃好了？……
還是再忍耐一下，把錢存下來呢？」

艾蜜莉非常地煩惱。

Emily tried to save up to buy a pretty doll,
but it was harder than she thought
because she had to say 'NO'
to snacks and beverages which she loved.

"Should I just give up on the pretty doll?……
Or should I be more patient and keep saving up?"

Emily struggled.

故事六 STORY 6

# 無價的珍珠
## Pearl of Great Price

天國又好像買賣人尋找好珠子，
遇見一顆重價的珠子，就去變賣他一切所有的，買了這顆珠子。
（馬太福音13：45－46）

有一位商人到處尋找品質最好的寶石。
「你們這裡沒有讓人眼睛一亮的寶石！」
「那麼……這個如何呢？」
「這個不行！我要找的寶石一定是要完美無瑕的。」

There was a merchant looking for the best jewelry.
"There's no extraordinary jewelry in your place!"
"Then...... how about this one?"
"No! The jewelry I'm looking for must be perfect and flawless."

寶石商人為了尋找最好的寶石，
不惜登上最險峻的山嶺，
或是前往最寒冷的國家，甚至在沙漠中迷失過，
但他從來不曾放棄過。

The merchart wanted the best jewelry,
even it meant that he had to walk over a very high and steep mountain,
through the coldest country or to get lost in a desert to find the jewel,
he never gave up.

有一天，寶石商人來到一個景色優美的海邊小鎮。
他在一間小珠寶店裡閒逛的時候，突然間，他的眼睛為之一亮。

One day, the merchant visited a village by a beautiful seashore.
While he was browsing through the jewels in a small store,
suddenly, something caught his attention.

「這該不會就是……？我可以再仔細地看看這顆珍珠嗎？」
當店主把這顆大珍珠拿給寶石商人看時，寶石商人用顫抖的雙手捧起它。
「**這實在太完美了！**看看這光彩鮮艷的色澤和形狀！這就是我一直找尋最好的寶石啊！」
商人的心激動地撲通撲通跳著，而他的臉也變得像蘋果一樣紅通通的。

"Is……is this…? Can I take a look at this pearl?"
When the owner handed over the huge pearl, the merchant's hands were shaking.
**"This is perfect!** Look at this glittering color and shape! This is exactly the one I have been looking for!"
His heart beat excitedly and his cheeks blushed like an apple.

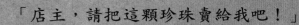

「店主，請把這顆珍珠賣給我吧！」
「你是說這顆珍珠嗎？它可是非常……非常昂貴的！
你買得起嗎？」
「我會想盡辦法把錢準備好的，我還會再回來的。」

"Sir, please sell this pearl to me!"
"Are you talking about this pearl?
This is a very, very expensive one!
Can you afford it?"
"I will do anything to get the money and come back."

商人急急忙忙地趕回家，為了籌錢買珍珠，他把自己所有的財產都變賣了。
「只為了區區一顆珍珠，竟然賣掉你所有的一切？
難道你瘋了嗎？你要三思而後行呀！
這可是你辛苦了一輩子，才賺來的錢呀！你再考慮考慮一下吧！」
商人的朋友們非常擔心，極力勸阻他，
但商人並沒有理會，他聽不進他們的勸告。

The merchant hurried home and started selling
all he had for the pearl.
"Are you selling all your property only for one pearl?
Are you crazy?"
"You should think again.
You spent your whole life to save up this much! Think twice."
The merchant's friends got worried, so they tried to stop him.
But he didn't listen, nor did he took their advice.

商人毫不猶豫地賣了自己全部的家當，
就跑去買珍珠。

He sold all he had without hesitation
and went to buy the pearl.

71

「這是買珍珠的錢！」
「嗯⋯⋯這些錢還差很多呢！」
「但這已是我所有的財產，也是我一生的積蓄了。」

寶石商人失望的眼神打動了店主的心。
「看在你為了它帶來所有財產的份上，
再加上你很識貨，知道這顆珍珠的價值，
我就賣給你吧！」

"Here is the money for the pearl!"
"Hmm… This is far from enough."
"But this is all I have. All that I saved."

The owner saw the desperation in the merchant's eyes, so he changed his mind.
"Knowing what you've done to buy this pearl,
I think you are the one who truly knows the value of it.
I will sell it to you!"

「嗚……哇！我簡直不敢相信，我終於得到了這顆珍珠！」
寶石商人開心到嘴都合不攏了。
他快樂的心情彷彿得到了全世界一樣。

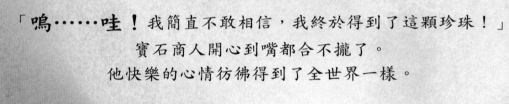

**"Wh-o-o-o-o-oa!** I can't believe I finally have it!"
The merchant couldn't keep his mouth closed.
He was so happy as if he had gotten the whole world.

「艾蜜莉，
作業都寫完了嗎？
讓媽媽檢查一下。」

"Emily,
did you finish your homework?
Let I check!" .

「嗯……
那個，我不是很了解，
所以就隨便做了。」

"Umm…
I was not sure how to do it,
so I just wrote whatever."

媽媽就對艾蜜莉說了一個
故事，藉此讓她知道基礎
的重要性。

Emily's mother told her a story
to let her know how important
a good foundation is.

# 沙土或磐石
## Sand or Rock

「所以,凡聽見我這話就去行的,好比一個聰明人,把房子蓋在磐石上;
雨淋,水沖,風吹,撞著那房子,房子總不倒塌,因為根基立在磐石上。
凡聽見我這話不去行的,好比一個無知的人,把房子蓋在沙土上;
雨淋、水沖、風吹,撞著那房子,房子就倒塌了,並且倒塌得很大。」
(馬太福音7:24—27)

「嘿！朋友，我們來比一比看誰的房子蓋得比較好！」
「好啊！就算你不說，我也有一些想法。」
「我也是！那麼我們現在就開始吧！」

這兩個比鄰而居的木匠朋友，就開始建造起他們心目中夢想的房子了。

"Hey buddy, let's see who builds the better house!"
"That sounds fun! I actually have some ideas already."
"Me too! Then let's get started!"

Two neighbors who were carpenters started building their own dream houses.

「好了，這裡就是我要建造夢想中美麗房子的地方！」
一個木匠看上了海邊，因為他被眼前湛藍的海水和美麗的風景深深吸引了。
儘管那是塊沙地，但是他也不在意，
只因眼前的風景實在太美了！

"Okay, I'm going to start building my beautiful dream house right here!"
One carpenter settled near the seashore where the blue ocean and the beautiful view caught his attention.
There was only sand all around, but he didn't give a second thought
because the view was awesome!

另一個木匠決定在山頂的岩石上蓋房屋。
「嗯！它看起來非常堅固。我要蓋一間世界上最堅固的房子！」

The other carpenter settled on the rock at the top of a hill.
"Umm. It seems very solid. I'm going to build the strongest house ever!"

刮刮刮⋯⋯叩叩叩⋯⋯咚咚咚⋯⋯砰砰砰！

幾個月後，敲敲打打的聲音結束，房子終於蓋好了。

「哇嗚！房子真的太漂亮了！
我也想住在這樣的房子裡！」
人們紛紛圍著這棟蓋在海邊的房子讚嘆不已。
和山坡頂上的那間房子相比，
人們更喜歡這棟蓋在海邊的房子，
因為它是一棟有著漂亮美景的房子。

## Scrape-scrape-scrape! Pound-pound-pound!

A few months passed and they finished building the houses.

"Wow! That's a beautiful house!
I want to live in that kind of house!"
People gathered around the house by the seashore and gave compliments.
Everyone there preferred the house by the seashore
to the one on the hill because of the beautiful scenery.

「嘿！看來這次的比賽，是我的房子贏了！哈哈哈！」
「是啊！我必須承認你蓋的房子比我的還漂亮多了。」
把房子蓋在岩石上的木匠，承認自己輸了。

"Hey! I think I won this competition. Ha-ha-ha!"
"Yes, I have to agree that your house is much prettier than mine,"
the carpenter who built the house on the hill admitted.

颼颼……瑟瑟……呼呼……颶颶！
有一天，天空突然刮起了呼嘯的大風，
一大片的烏雲慢慢地飄了過來。

**Whoosh, whoosh. Whizz, whizz.**
One day, it got so windy
and dark clouds approached slowly.

**隆隆⋯⋯轟轟⋯⋯隆隆⋯⋯轟轟！**

一陣閃電交雜轟隆巨響的雷聲後，一個令人害怕的超級暴風來了！

天空就下起了可怕的狂風暴雨。

天空裂開，就好像一個關不住的水龍頭，大雨傾盆而下，

樹木被連根拔起，而滾滾洪水橫掃了海邊的小鎮。

**瀝瀝⋯⋯淅淅⋯⋯瀝瀝⋯⋯淅淅！**

蓋在海邊的漂亮房子，在狂風暴雨中不停搖晃著。

住在裡面的木匠嚇得從漂亮的房子裡跑了出來。

### Flash- flash! Rumble, boom, boom!

After the lightening struck and the thunder roared, a big, scary storm came.

The sky broke open and it rained heavily like an open faucet.

Some tree roots were plucked out by the strong wind.

The floodwaters swept through the village and along the seashore.

### Splash-splash, whistling-whistling.

The pretty house by the seashore began to be shaken by the strong wind.

The carpenter living in the house quickly ran out in fear.

**嘰嘰……喳喳！啁啁……啾啾！**

不知何時，明亮的太陽再度映照在小鎮上，鳥兒們開心地飛來飛去。

整晚都提心吊膽的木匠，一等到天氣放晴，就馬上慌慌張張地跑回去看他的房子。
「喔……我的天呀！我的房子呢？我的房子……我的房子到哪裡去了？」
經過暴風雨整夜地摧殘，房子完全杳無蹤影！

另一方面，建造在山頂上的房子卻沒有受到任何損害，依然很堅固地待在原地。
「哎！要是我也把房子建在磐石上就好了！」

**Tweet-tweet-tweet!**

Later, the sun came out, shining down on the village and the birds flew happily.

The carpenter was worried all night, so as soon as the weather got better, he ran to his house nervously.
"Oh, NO! Where is my house? Where did it go?"
The house was completely destroyed by the storm the night before!

On the other hand, the house on the rock at the top of the hill remained there, standing still.
"Urgh! I should have built my house on the rock, too!"

媽媽：艾蜜莉，現在要刷牙囉！
艾蜜莉：等一下！
媽媽：艾蜜莉，現在不是練琴的時間嗎？
艾蜜莉：等一下啦！
媽媽：吃飯囉！
艾蜜莉：等一下啦！
媽媽：艾蜜莉，妳可以來這裡一下嗎？
　　　媽媽有事要告訴妳。
艾蜜莉：晚點再講，不行嗎？
媽媽：不行！就是現在。

**Mommy:** Emily. It's time to brush your teeth!
**Emily:** Just a second!
**Mommy:** Emily, it's time to practice the piano now.
**Emily:** Later!
**Mommy:** Time to eat!
**Emily:** One more minute.
**Mommy:** Emily, can you come here for a second?
　　　　　I have something to tell you.
**Emily:** Can we do this later?
**Mommy:** No! It has to be right now.

# 富人和拉撒路
## The Rich Man and Lazarus

「有一個財主穿著紫色袍和細麻布衣服，天天奢華宴樂。
又有一個討飯的，名叫拉撒路，渾身生瘡，被人放在財主門口，
要得財主桌子上掉下來的零碎充飢，並且狗來舔他的瘡。
後來那討飯的死了，被天使帶去放在亞伯拉罕的懷裡。財主也死了，並且埋葬了。
他在陰間受痛苦，舉目遠遠地望見亞伯拉罕，又望見拉撒路在他懷裡，
就喊著說：『我祖亞伯拉罕哪，可憐我吧！打發拉撒路來，用指頭尖蘸點水，涼涼我的舌頭；因為我在這火焰裡，極其痛苦。』
亞伯拉罕說：『兒啊，你該回想你生前享過福，拉撒路也受過苦；如今他在這裡得安慰，你倒受痛苦。
不但這樣，並且在你我之間，有深淵限定，以致人要從這邊過到你們那邊是不能的；要從那邊過到我們這邊也是不能的。』
財主說：『我祖啊！既是這樣，求你打發拉撒路到我父家去；
因為我還有五個弟兄，他可以對他們作見證，免得他們也來到這痛苦的地方。』
亞伯拉罕說：『他們有摩西和先知的話可以聽從。』
他說：『我祖亞伯拉罕哪，不是的，若有一個從死裡復活的，到他們那裡去的，他們必要悔改。』
亞伯拉罕說：『若不聽從摩西和先知的話，就是有一個從死裡復活的，他們也是不聽勸。』」
**（路加福音16：19－31）**

在一個村莊裡，有一棟金碧輝煌的房子。
住在裡面的富豪，每天都會舉辦宴會和朋友們一起玩樂。

在房子的大門旁邊，住著一個叫拉撒路的乞丐。
拉撒路靠著從富豪家裡丟棄的食物來填飽肚子。
富豪看拉撒路患有嚴重的皮膚病，樣子很可怕，想要趕走他，
但是除了忍耐也沒有別的辦法，因為人們都稱讚他說：
「像那樣的乞丐你都不趕走他，你真是心胸寬大的人啊！」

There was a magnificently splendid house in a village.
The rich owner invited his friends to his party and had fun every day.

In front of the entrance of the house, there lived a homeless man named Lazarus.
Lazarus lived off the food thrown out from the luxurious house.
The rich man wanted to chase the homeless man out from his property because of his scary appearance.
But he couldn't do anything about him because people passing by always complimented the rich man by saying,
"You never kick the homeless away, you are such a generous person!"

住在大門旁邊的拉撒路，雖然常常感到又餓又冷的，
但是他的臉上總是帶著開朗的微笑。

「謝謝你的幫助，祝你長命百歲！」
「老人家，祝你福運亨通！」

人們都因為拉撒路清亮的聲音，心情變得很愉快，
甚至有些人看到拉撒路後，反而得到了勇氣。

Lazarus, who sat at the front entrance suffered from hunger and cold very offen,
but he always had a smile on his face.

"Thank you for your help. May you live a long and healthy life!"
"May God bless you, Sir."

The joyful voice of Lazarus often made people feel happy when they passed by.
Some people even got encouraged just by looking at Lazarus.

拉撒路也對豪宅的主人說：
「先生，非常謝謝你，願上帝多多賜福給你。」
然而富豪一點也不領情。
他是一個有錢有勢又非常傲慢的人。

Lazarus also said to the rich man,
"Sir, thank you. May God bless you abundantly."
However, the rich man always snubbed him.
He was a very arrogant man who only believed in his own wealth and power.

有一天，富豪和拉撒路都死了。
死後富豪落在熊熊的烈火中感到非常痛苦。
就在那時，富豪看到了拉撒路，他居然就在對面的天國裡，
於是富豪大聲喊叫說：

One day, both the rich man and Lazarus died.
The rich man was thrown into the fire and was in much pain.
Right at that moment, he saw Lazarus way over on the opposite side in the heaven,
so he shouted,

「我的先祖亞伯拉罕！
請你派拉撒路帶些水來給我喝！」
可是，拉撒路沒有辦法到富豪那裡去，
富豪也不能來到天國這裡。

"Father of Abraham!
Please send Lazarus to give me some water!"
But Lazarus could not reach the rich man,
and neither could the rich man get to heaven.

97

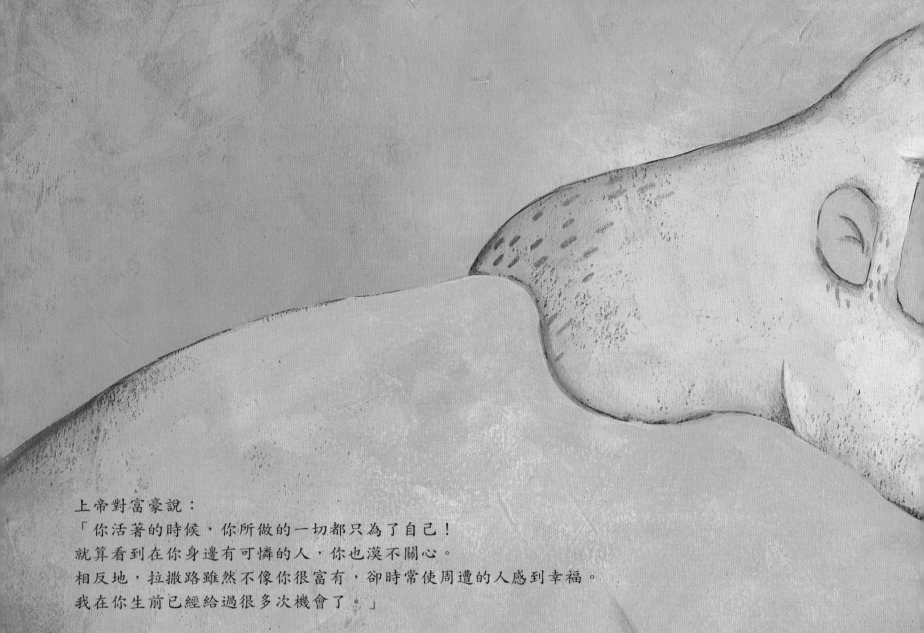

上帝對富豪說：
「你活著的時候，你所做的一切都只為了自己！
就算看到在你身邊有可憐的人，你也漠不關心。
相反地，拉撒路雖然不像你很富有，卻時常使周遭的人感到幸福。
我在你生前已經給過很多次機會了。」

God said to the rich man,
"When you were alive, you were selfish.
You didn't take care of the poor around you.
Lazarus, on the contrary, though he was not rich, he made people around him happy.
I give you many chances while you were alive."

天色漸漸暗了，
艾蜜莉躲了起來不敢回家，
因為她做錯了事，
害怕回家以後會被罵。

It was dark outside, but Emily was hiding and afraid to go home because she had done something wrong and she was worried about being scolded.

「艾蜜莉啊！你在哪裡？艾蜜莉！」
「這裡也沒有看見。去別的地方找吧！」
爸爸、媽媽因為找不到艾蜜莉，
就轉向別的地方去了。

"Emily! Where are you? Emily!"
"I don't think she is here, let's look somewhere else."
Her mommy and daddy couldn't find her, so they walked away.

「媽媽！我在這裡啊！」
"Mommy! I'm here!"

媽媽淚流滿面的將艾蜜莉緊緊地擁在懷中。
Emily's mother, who was sobbing, hugged Emily tightly in her arms.

# 浪子回頭
## The Prodigal Son

小兒子對父親說：「父親，請你把我應得的家業分給我。」他父親就把產業分給他們。

過了不多幾日，小兒子就把他一切所有的都收拾起來，往遠方去了。在那裡任意放蕩，浪費資財。

既耗盡了一切所有的，又遇著那地方大遭饑荒，就窮苦起來。

於是去投靠那地方的一個人；那人打發他到田裡去放豬。

他恨不得拿豬所吃的豆莢充飢，也沒有人給他。

他醒悟過來，就說：「我父親有多少的雇工，口糧有餘，我倒在這裡餓死嗎？

我要起來，到我父親那裡去，向他說：父親！我得罪了天，又得罪了你；

從今以後，我不配稱為你的兒子，把我當作一個雇工吧！」

於是起來，往他父親那裡去。相離還遠，他父親看見，就動了慈心，跑去抱著他的頸項，連連與他親嘴。

兒子說：「父親！我得罪了天，又得罪了你；從今以後，我不配稱為你的兒子。」

父親卻吩咐僕人說：「把那上好的袍子快拿出來給他穿；把戒指戴在他指頭上；把鞋穿在他腳上；

把那肥牛犢牽來宰了，我們可以吃喝快樂；

因為我這個兒子是死而復活，失而又得的。」他們就快樂起來。

（路加福音15:11－24）

一對夫婦有兩個兒子，
懶惰的小兒子，總是令他的爸爸媽媽操心。
有一天他很沒有禮貌地對父親說：
「爸爸，把屬於我的財產先給我吧！
反正，你死了以後，還不是要給我，對吧？」

父親雖然傷心，但心裡經過一番掙扎後，就把財產給他了。
「耶！太棒了！我馬上就要離開這煩死人的家了！」
小兒子就往遠方的城市出發了。

A couple had two sons,
and the younger son was so lazy and made his parents worried all the time.
One day he came to his father and said rudely,
"Father, let me have my portion of the property!
When you pass away, it will become mine anyway, right?"

The father was hurt but after he struggled, he decided to give his son his property.
"Yes! I'm going to leave this annoying home right now!"
Then he left for a faraway city.

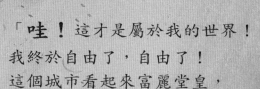

「哇！這才是屬於我的世界！
我終於自由了，自由了！
這個城市看起來富麗堂皇，
如果我住在這裡生活應該會多采多姿吧！」

"**Wow!** This is the world I belong to.
I'm free at last. Free as a bird!
This city is gorgeous.
How nice it will be if I can live here!"

小兒子隨心所欲地大手筆亂花錢。
「告訴我你們想要什麼，今天也是我請客！」
「你果然太帥了！」壞朋友們用甜言蜜語去奉承他。
小兒子早就把他的家人拋在腦後了。

但是父親每天開著門，站在門旁邊等著小兒子回家。

The younger son started to spend all he had.
"Tell me what you want and I will pay it for you. It's all on me!"
"You are the best!" Bad friends flattered him with beautiful words.
He completely forgot about his family.

But the father always kept the door open, waiting for his younger son.

有一天，那個地方發生大饑荒。錢花光光的小兒子，不但變成窮光蛋，還落得養豬的下場了。
他餓到要搶豬的食物吃，並且睡在豬群中。

「父親！」豆大的淚水簌簌地掉下來。
「在我父親的家裡連僕人們都不愁吃穿，如果我回去當僕人的話，父親願意接受我嗎？
唉！不管了，先回家再說吧！」

One day there was a famine. And the younger son spent all he had.
He had no choice but to take care of pigs in order to feed himself.
Sometimes, he was so starved that he had to steal the pigs' food and sleep among them.

"Father!" He cried with teary eyes.
"Even the servants are well-fed and well-dressed at my father's house.
If I am willing to be one of his servants, would he accept me?
Anyway, I have to go home first!"

太陽漸漸西下，所有的影子也慢慢地拉長了。
一天又要過去了。
總是站在門外，等待兒子回來的父親，
「唉……什麼時候他才會回來呢？」他長長地嘆了一口氣。

這時，望著遠方道路的父親突然停了下來，
「那是誰？我的兒子？沒錯！他一定是我的兒子！」

The sun was going down and the shadows lengthened.
Days passed.
As always, the father was waiting for his son outside.
"When will he come back?" He sighed.

Suddenly, he froze as he looked at the road far away.
"Who is that? My son? Yes! That must be my son!"

不管他變得多髒、多像乞丐，
父親一眼就認出他來了。
「沒錯！兒子！是我的兒子！」
父親慌忙地朝著兒子奔去。

Even though the son looked like a dirty beggar,
the father recognized him at once.
**"Son! My Son!"**
He ran to his son.

父親抱著兒子哭了很長的一段時間。
「父親，我錯了！我真是一個愚蠢的人。這一切都是我的錯。」
「沒關係，兒子！我很高興你終於回來了！」

父親脫下自己的外袍，把它披在兒子身上。
「大家一起來吧！看我的兒子回來了！我要舉行歡迎會吧！哈哈哈！」
空氣中充滿著歡樂的笑聲。

The father hugged his son tight and cried for a long time.
"Father, I'm sorry! I was such a fool. It's all my fault."
"That's okay son. I'm glad you are back."

The father took off his robe and put it on his son.
"Everyone! Look! My son is back! Let's have a party! Hahaha!"
Joyful laughter filled in the air.

秋收
辛勤的農夫在小麥田裡認真工作著，
到了收割季節，
黃澄澄的麥田隨風搖曳真美麗！

112

請你來找找看：

3隻麻雀
10根稗子
1隻糞金龜
6隻蚯蚓
5隻螞蟻
1位農夫

113

前頁解答